Decorated by Design

Returning to the Beauty Within

By
Sahibzada

Copyright © *Sahibzada*, 2025
All Rights Reserved

This book is subject to the condition that no part of this book is to be reproduced, transmitted in any form or means; electronic or mechanical, stored in a retrieval system, photocopied, recorded, scanned, or otherwise. Any of these actions require the proper written permission of the author.

Table of Contents

Introduction 1

Chapter 1: The Instinct to Decorate 2

Chapter 2: When Expression Becomes Etching 4

Chapter 3: Designed Already – The Divine Blueprint 6

Chapter 4: Islam & the Art of Clothing 9

Chapter 5: The Psychology of Return 12

Chapter 6: Bare, but Not Lost 14

Chapter 7: Covered in Light 17

Chapter 8: Decorated by Design — Returning to the Beauty Within 20

To every soul searching for beauty outside -

May you remember:

you were already decorated within.

Introduction

We are all born with a need — not just to exist, but to be seen.

To feel beautiful. To be recognized. To express what words sometimes cannot say.

And somewhere along the path of life, we begin to decorate. With clothes, colours, accessories... and sometimes — with permanent marks on the body.

But this book is not a judgment. It is a reminder.

That even before you touched your skin, God had already decorated you. Not with ink or metal, but with meaning. With symmetry. With soul.

The journey ahead is not about guilt. It's about guidance.

Whether you are marked, unmarked, wondering, or healing — this book welcomes you.

It holds space for your questions and offers a quiet return to your original design — beautiful, intentional, whole.

Read slowly. Reflect deeply. May each chapter bring you closer to your inner beauty and to the
One who designed you by purpose.

—Sahibzada

Chapter 1: The Instinct to Decorate

Humans are not just made to live – we are made to express. To exist beautifully. To be seen with meaning. And to carry an outer reflection of our inner truth.

This is not ego. This is not vanity. It is fitrah – the natural design of the soul.

From the very beginning, humans adorned themselves. With leaves, fabrics, metals, colors, patterns... Not to hide, but to highlight.

Every culture, every age, every land – they all decorated themselves. Because decoration is not modern – it is eternal. A whisper from within that says: *'Let me be seen in a way that reflects who I am.'*

That's why a child smiles when you dress them in something beautiful. That's why adults stand taller in clothes that feel like them. That's why we choose colours that match our moods. Because the body is a canvas – and the soul wants to paint.

But not all decoration is light. Some come from pain. From brokenness. From a craving not to express the soul... but to fill the silence.

And this is where the instinct to decorate begins to shift – from celebration... to compensation.

When beauty becomes burden, and silence feels like emptiness, the human soul searches for something more permanent – something to hold the weight of feeling seen.

And in that moment, the skin becomes a journal. A place to write pain, memory, meaning, rebellion, or love. This is where tattooing begins – not always as rebellion. . . but often as a misguided form of remembrance.

But the truth remains:

You were already decorated... by the One who made you with no flaws in your form and no need for edits.

Chapter 2:
When Expression Becomes Etching

There's a moment in every soul's journey when the desire to decorate turns into the desire to define.

When clothing no longer feels enough. When fabric becomes too temporary. When you want something etched – not worn.

That's when the skin becomes a journal. Not to show beauty... but to show a story the world didn't take the time to listen to.

A scar disguised as art. A cry disguised as ink. A silent rebellion, or sometimes... a silent plea. Many think tattooing is just defiance. But often, it's remembrance.

A name, a date, a symbol – things the soul doesn't want to forget. So it burns them into the flesh as if to say:

"Even if the world forgets, I won't."

But remembrance doesn't need to be written on the skin – because the heart is the true vessel of memory. And the mind – when at peace – remembers without scars.

For some, tattooing is about control. When life feels chaotic, we choose where the needle lands. We decide what goes on in our body. We become, for a brief moment, the author of our own image.

But this control is temporary. Because no ink can rewrite the soul. And no design can remove the ache of feeling unseen... unheard... or forgotten.

The soul already came with a mark. A purpose. A design.

Every fingerprint is unique—not because of randomness, but because of intent.

God, the Creator of beauty, has written His signs into our very bodies — from the curve of the eye to the strength in our hands.

You are already tattooed by divine design. You just haven't looked deep enough to see it.

Chapter 3: Designed Already – The Divine Blueprint

Before you ever wore a shirt, before your skin ever touched fabric, you were already designed. Not by trend. Not by culture. But by the Divine Hand that makes no mistake.

Look at your fingerprint – no two on earth match it. Look at the curve of your ears, the symmetry in your eyes, the architecture of your bones... you are not random. You are written.

In the womb, before you took shape, God already knew your name. Before your body was seen by the world, it was known – fully and intimately – by the One who formed it.

So when you think of marking your body, pause and remember:

You are not a blank canvas. You are a scroll... Already filled with divine detail.

To alter that design – to rewrite what was perfected – is not freedom. It is forgetfulness.

In the Qur'an, God says: *"And in yourselves — do you not see?" (Surah Adh-Dhariyat 51:21)*

Your body is an ayah. A verse. A sign of divine perfection. It breathes, heals, breaks, rebuilds — all without your command.

So when we add tattoos, what are we saying?

Are we improving His design? Are we adding beauty to what He already called "Ahsan Taqweem"

the most perfect form?

No. We are answering pain with a pen that was never meant for skin.

Fitrah is your original state. It is your blueprint. And God does not build anything in need of fixing.

He allows you to decorate — yes. But not by changing the body. He guides you to decorate through what you wear… because that allows the body to remain sacred. God doesn't reject beauty. He protects it. By teaching us:

"You are already enough."

"You don't need to be rewritten — you just need to be remembered."

Chapter 4:
Islam & the Art of Clothing

Islam never denied your urge to decorate — it simply redirected it.

The desire to express beauty, to design, to be seen with grace — that's not forbidden. It's understood. God, the Designer of all things, knew His creation would long for beauty. So He didn't suppress it...

He guided it.

That's why Islam emphasizes clothing — not just as protection but as expression through intention. What you wear is not about hiding. It's about honouring.

Islamic clothing doesn't strip you of identity. It shapes it. It invites you to design yourself with dignity, presence, and poise.

Silk, linen, wool, embroidery, jewels — Islam doesn't deny aesthetics. It elevates them. It invites you to wrap your body in meaning so your body itself remains untouched, sacred, and whole.

In Islam:

Clothes are not a cover of shame. They are a sign of worth.

When you decorate your clothes, you fulfil the same natural urge that tattooing tries to answer — but without the permanence, without the pain, and without rewriting what God has already perfected.

That's why God tells us in the Qur'an: *"O children of Adam, We have bestowed upon you clothing to conceal your private parts and as adornment..."* *(Surah Al-A'raf 7:26)*

Adornment. That means the need is not ignored — it is embraced.

You were meant to be beautiful. But the beauty Islam offers is not based on skin... It's based on presence.
In Islam, your identity isn't in ink — it's in how you walk, how you speak, and how you wrap your soul in outer expression.

That's why the cloak, the jilbab, the turban, the thobe — just these alone are not Islamic clothing.

They are expressions of modesty from certain cultures, yes — but Islam doesn't confine beauty to one style or tradition.

God gave us principles, not restrictions.

For men and women, those principles include modesty, dignity, covering of awrah, and avoidance of arrogance or imitation of the opposite gender.

Any clothing – in any culture – that fulfils those principles becomes Islamic in spirit.

So your beauty doesn't need to look like someone else's. Your dignity doesn't need to match a trend. And your Islamic identity can shine through any fabric that reflects those divine boundaries.

Chapter 5:
The Psychology of Return

No one wakes up one day and decides to tattoo their body.

It begins long before — in the mind, in the heart, in the quiet corners of the self that feel unseen or incomplete.

We reach for ink when words no longer feel enough. We mark the skin when emotions go unwitnessed. We decorate the body because we've forgotten how to decorate the soul.

But returning is not about shame. It's about remembrance.

Tattooing often masks itself as empowerment: *"I'm claiming my body."* But in truth, we tattoo when we feel disconnected from it.

We try to build identity through symbols, shapes, pain, or permanence because we've lost the deeper sense of belonging. Not belonging to society… but to ourselves. To God. To our original form.

That form still exists — untouched beneath the ink.

You don't need to erase the tattoo. You need to heal the belief.

The return doesn't start at the laser clinic. It starts in the mindset. You don't need to punish your past. You need to understand it.

Ask:

- *Why did I mark myself?*

- *What was I trying to say?*

- *What am I ready to release now?*

Because when the need disappears, the ink loses its power.

True return is not physical first — it is psychological. A shift in how you see yourself... and a return to how God sees you.

Chapter 6:
Bare, but Not Lost

Honouring the Soul Beneath the Ink

You may carry tattoos.

You may have chosen markings in the past.

When the pain felt louder than, peace, and ink felt safer than silence.

But let this be said, with love and clarity:

You are not lost,

You are not damaged,

You are not beyond return.

You are simply someone who tried to speak, when no one else was listening.

And now,

You've remembered your voice.

The Tattoo is Not Who You Are

It may live on your skin.

But it does not define your worth. Not to your Creator. Not to your future.

Not to your ability to return with full dignity and grace.

In fact, the act of turning back,

With ink on your body and sincerity in your heart,

Is honoured.

Because it is harder, Because it is real.
And because God sees what's beneath the skin,
Before anyone else sees what's on it.

No Shame in the Journey

You didn't mark your body in sin,

You marked it in search.

And now that you've found the truth… You don't need to erase the past.
You need to reclaim it.

Let your tattoos become reminders,

Not of rebellion,
But of redemption.

Let them say,

"This was once my pain,

But now, it's just part of my story,

Not my identity."

Covered in Grace

You may not be able to remove the mark,
but you can remove the meaning.
You can reclaim your self-worth.

You can return to honouring your body, your presence, your soul.

You can still walk into any gathering,
Into any prayer,
Into any life,

Fully welcomed by God.

Because He is not watching the ink.
He is watching the intention.

And when your heart returns, so does your light.

Chapter 7: Covered in Light

The Radiance of Dignity and Inner Beauty

In a world obsessed with exposure,
choosing to cover is an act of power.
A quiet revolution,
A bold return to dignity over display.

Because when you dress with intention,

Not to attract
Attention, but to
Protect value.
You are not hiding.

You are shining.

Light Is Not What You Show – It's What You Carry

Modesty is not restriction.
It is recognition.
That you are already valuable,
Already beautiful,

Already whole.

You don't have to reveal
everything,
To be respected.
You don't have to bare your body
to express your soul.

God says:
"And tell the believing men and women to lower their gaze and guard their modesty…" Because purity begins in the eyes before it ever touches the fabric.

True Beauty Has Weight

Real beauty isn't loud.
It's not desperate.
It doesn't demand attention,
it commands it.

The person who walks in covered
grace,
Enters the room like a lantern,
Not burning bright,
But glowing steady.
With humility. With presence. With peace.

That's what modesty gives you:
Weight without noise.
Elegance without exposure.
Presence without performance.

The Body is a Temple — and Light Deserves Shelter

When you know your worth,
You don't display it freely.
You don't decorate yourself for consumption,
You design yourself for purpose.

Every fold of fabric becomes a prayer,
Every choice to cover becomes a candle lit in a world,
Starving for truth.
You are not hiding your beauty,
You are placing it where it belongs.

Within the protection of light,
Within the purpose of your creation.

Because what is sacred,
Is always guarded… not exposed.

Chapter 8: Decorated by Design — Returning to the Beauty Within

Returning to the Beauty Within

You were never empty,
Never plain.
Never incomplete.

From the first breath,
You were already enough.
Written, shaped, and presented,
By the greatest artist of all time.

God made no mistake.

Every curve,
Every shade.
Every detail of your form
was intentional.

But in the noise of the world,

In the pressure to be seen,
We forgot.

We tried to add, edit, mark, pierce, and ink,
thinking beauty was something to be achieved,
rather than something to be remembered.

Your Soul Never Needed Saving – Just Remembering
This book was not written to judge those who marked themselves.
It was written to remind the ones who forgot
that they were always marked by purpose.

Not with ink,
But with intention.
Not with scars.
But with soul.

You are already decorated by design.
And when you understand that,
You stop trying to prove your,
beauty and start protecting it.

You dress with dignity.
You walk with grace.
You express,
Not to please the

World...

But to honour your truth.

A Final Whisper

To the one who still wonders ...
Who still feels "less than"...
Who still carries the past like a tattoo on the heart.

You are seen.
You are chosen.
You are beautiful.
Just as you were made.

Return not to perfection,

But to your natural state.

The fitrah,
The soul that smiles from within.
The self that doesn't need to scream to be noticed.

This is the true art of being.

You are not missing decoration.
You are the decoration.
A living reminder that design – when divine – needs no addition.

So cover yourself in meaning.
Live with presence.
And shine not by being loud…

… but by being real.

You are — and always have been -•
Decorated by Design.

www.ingramcontent.com/pod-product-compliance
Lightning Source LLC
Chambersburg PA
CBHW061146170426
43209CB00011B/1574

THE CHURCH
WITHOUT WALLS

APPLYING EARLY CHURCH MODEL TO MODERN ERA

Copyright 2023 (Richard Okunade) –All rights reserved.

The content contained within this book may not be reproduced, duplicated, or transmitted without direct written permission from the author or the publisher.

Under no circumstances will any blame or legal responsibility be held against the publisher, or author, for any damages, reparation, or monetary loss due to the information contained within this book, either directly or indirectly.

This book is based on Church Without Walls, Applying Early Church Model To Modern Era. It is copyright protected and is only for personal use. The content contained within this book may not be reproduced, duplicated, or transmitted without direct written permission from the author or publisher.

There is no blame or legal responsibility for any damages, reparation, or monetary loss due to the information contained within the book.

Legal Notice:

This book is copyright protected. It is only for personal use. You cannot amend, distribute, sell, use, quote, or paraphrase any part, or the content within this book, without the author's or publisher's consent.
This book is based on Church Without Walls, Applying Early Church Model To

Modern Era.

Disclaimer Notice:

Please note the information contained within this document is for educational and informational purposes only. All effort has been executed to present accurate, up-to-date, reliable, and complete information. No warranties of any kind are declared or implied. Readers acknowledge that the author is not engaged in rendering legal, financial, medical, or professional advice.The content within this book has been derived from various sources.Please consult a licensed professional before attempting any techniques outlined in this book.

By reading this document, the reader agrees that under no circumstances is the author responsible for any direct or indirect losses incurred because of the use of the information contained within this document, including, but not limited to, errors, omissions,or inaccuracies.

Dedication

I dedicate this book to the loving memory of my late father, whose presence and guidance shaped my early years and instilled in me a love for learning and knowledge. Though he is no longer with us, his counsel continues to inspire and guide me.

To my beloved mother, whose unwavering love, sacrifice, and encouragement have been a constant source of strength throughout my life. Her nurturing and support have allowed me to pursue my passions and dreams.

To my darling wife and lovely three daughters, who bring joy, love, and inspiration into my life every day. Your unwavering belief in me and your endless support has been the driving force behind my endeavors.

And to Pastor Olusegun Omotayo, whose ministry I had the privilege to serve under for 10 transformative years. His mentorship, wisdom, and guidance have shaped my spiritual journey and equipped me for the task of sharing the message of faith and hope.

This book is dedicated to all these incredible individuals who have touched my life and played a significant role in shaping the person I am today. May their memories and contributions continue to inspire and bless others as we journey together in faith and love.

Author Biography

Richard Okunade is an ordained Deacon well-known for his outstanding ability to teach the Bible with clarity and profound theological insights. Richard Okunade, who has over a decade of experience as a Bible Teacher leader within a local church, has played an important part in allowing countless individuals to dive deeper into scripture and nourish their faith.

Richard Okunade, a respected Bible teacher, has also served as a preacher in numerous churches, actively promoting the growth and development of emerging congregations. His unrelenting drive to build strong and linked online communities, inspired by Christ's love and a strong commitment to service, has compelled him to interact with social media platforms. Richard Okunade hopes to reach a wider audience through these channels beyond the traditional constraints of physical church locations.

Thanks to his compelling and uplifting teaching method, Richard Okunade has emerged as a recognized voice within the internet community, motivating numerous individuals to live more purposeful and rewarding lives via their steadfast faith.

Table Of Content

Dedication ii
Author Biography iii
Table Of Content iv
INTRODUCTION 1
What Is The Church? 1
CHAPTER ONE: Introduction To Church Without Walls 3
    Definition Of A Church Without Walls 5
    Historical Background Of Church Without Walls 6
    Purpose Of The Study 7
CHAPTER TWO: Biblical Basis Of Church Without Walls 9
    The Great Commission 10
    The Ministry Of Jesus 12
    Learning From The Early Church Model 13
    Applying Early Church Model To Modern Era 15
CHAPTER THREE: Characteristics Of A Church Without Walls 17
    Openness To All 18
    Emphasis On Discipleship 19
    Use Of Technology 21
    Flexibility In Worship 22
    Social Justice And Outreach 23
CHAPTER FOUR: Benefits Of Church Without Walls 25

Table Of Content

    Accessibility 26

    Diversity 27

    Cost-Effective 28

    Community Building 29

CHAPTER FIVE: Challenges Of Church Without Walls 31

    Maintaining Relationships 32

    Providing Pastoral Care 34

    Financial Sustainability 35

    Accountability 36

CHAPTER SIX: Case Studies Of Church Without Walls 39

    Saddleback Online 40

    Life.Church 42

    Mennonite Online Fellowship 43

    St. Isidore's Episcopal Church 44

CHAPTER SEVEN: Impact Of Church Without Walls 46

    Increased Reach 47

    Changed Lives 48

    Community Impact 48

CHAPTER EIGHT: Future Of Church Without Walls 50

    Emerging Trends 51

    Opportunities 52

    Threats 54

Conclusion 56

References: 57

INTRODUCTION

What Is The Church?

- **Church in Greek:**

The Greek word for "church" is "ekklesia" (ἐκκλησία). In the New Testament, it is used to refer to the assembly or gathering of believers. The term carries the idea of a called-out group or an assembly of people who are brought together for a specific purpose. It is derived from the combination of the words "ek" (out of) and "kaleo" (to call).

The usage of "ekklesia" in the New Testament reflects the concept of the assembly of believers being called out from the world and brought into a relationship with God through Jesus Christ. It signifies the community of believers who are called out from the world and united in their faith and commitment to Christ.

- **Church as a collection of believers:**

The Church, as a collection of believers, refers to the community of individuals who have put their faith in Jesus Christ as their Lord and Savior. It is not limited to a specific physical location or institution but encompasses all believers worldwide who are united in their relationship with Christ.

This understanding of the Church emphasizes the spiritual unity of believers, regardless of their cultural or denominational differences. It highlights the shared identity and common purpose of believers as members of the body of Christ.

- **Church as an individual member of the body of Christ:**

The Church is also described as the body of Christ, with Jesus being the Head of the Church. This imagery emphasizes the interconnectedness and interdependence of believers within the larger body. Each individual believer is seen as a vital part of the body, contributing to its overall functioning and growth.

As an individual member of the body of Christ, each believer has a unique role and gifts to contribute to the collective mission of the Church. This understanding emphasizes the importance of unity, cooperation, and mutual support among believers in fulfilling the purposes of God.

CHAPTER ONE

Introduction To Church Without Walls

An Introduction to Church Without Walls is an overview of a church that exists beyond the physical walls of a traditional church building. This type of church is characterized by its emphasis on online platforms, social media, and other non-traditional means of connecting with members and reaching out to new people.

The idea of a Church Without Walls has its roots in the early Christian church, where worship and community building often took place in homes and other informal settings. However, with the rise of traditional church buildings and the centralization of religious institutions, the idea of a church beyond physical walls has gained renewed interest in recent years.

The purpose of a Church Without Walls is to create a welcoming and inclusive environment. Everyone may access it, regardless of their location, background, or age and circumstances. The idea is to instill a sense of belonging, community, and connection among members and reach out to individuals who might not feel at ease attending a traditional church.

A Church Without Walls is not a replacement for traditional churches but rather an alternative way of connecting with others and worshiping God. It provides a platform for people to unite in fellowship, prayer, and service, regardless of their physical location.

One of the key benefits of a Church Without Walls is its ability to reach new people who may not have been previously connected to a traditional church. With the use of technology and social media, these churches can connect with people around the world and provide them with opportunities to grow in their faith and connect with others who share their beliefs.

However, there are also challenges associated with a Church Without Walls. Maintaining relationships and providing pastoral care can be more difficult without the structure of a physical church building. Financial sustainability and accountability can also be challenges for these types of churches.

Overall, an Introduction to Church Without Walls overviews a modern approach to Christianity that seeks to break down barriers to worship and make people's lives more inclusive, accessible, and inviting of all backgrounds and circumstances.

Definition Of A Church Without Walls

A Church Without Walls is a modern approach to Christianity that seeks to break down barriers to worship and create a more inclusive, accessible, and inviting place for individuals from all walks of life and circumstances. This type of church is characterized by its emphasis on online platforms, social media, and other non-traditional means of connecting with members and reaching out to new people.

Unlike traditional churches, a Church Without Walls has no physical building as its primary gathering place. Instead, it relies on technology and other means to connect people and create community. This approach allows people who may not be able to attend a traditional church due to geographic location, health issues, or other reasons to participate in worship and fellowship.

A Church Without Walls's primary focus is building relationships with God and others. Members of these churches typically emphasize the importance of discipleship and spiritual growth, as well as engaging in social justice and outreach activities to positively impact their communities.

One of the key benefits of a Church Without Walls is its accessibility. People can participate in worship and community events as long as they have internet access from anywhere in the world. This makes it easier for people who live in rural areas, those who are homebound, or those who have other barriers to traditional worship to connect with others and grow in their faith.

However, there are also challenges associated with a Church Without Walls. Maintaining relationships and providing pastoral care can be more difficult without the structure of a physical church building. Financial sustainability and accountability can also be challenges for these types of churches.

Overall, a Church Without Walls offers a unique approach to worship and community building that has the potential to reach new people and make a positive impact on the world.

Historical Background Of Church Without Walls

Throughout history, movements and groups have emphasized the importance of a church that exists beyond physical walls. For example, the Quakers, known as the Society of Friends, have historically been known for their decentralized worship and community-building approach. Quaker meetings often occur in homes, community centers, and other non-traditional spaces.

In the early 20th century, the Pentecostal movement emerged, emphasizing the Holy Spirit's importance and the personal experience of God's presence. Pentecostal churches often prioritize emotional, participatory worship experiences and may use non-traditional spaces for gatherings.

More recently, the rise of technology and social media has made it possible for churches to connect with members and reach out to new people beyond physical walls. Online worship services, social media groups, and other digital platforms have allowed people to participate in worship and community events from anywhere in the world.

Today, many churches identify as Church Without Walls, each with a unique approach to worship, community building, and outreach. Some churches may use technology and social media to connect with members, while others may prioritize in-person gatherings in non-traditional spaces.

Overall, the historical background of Church Without Walls is rooted in the early Christian church and has been shaped by various movements and groups throughout history. Today, technology and social media have enabled this concept to thrive and provide a new way of worshiping and connecting with others in the modern world.

Purpose Of The Study

The purpose of studying Church Without Walls is to explore the concept of a church that exists beyond physical walls and to understand its implications for modern Christianity. This study seeks to provide a comprehensive understanding of the Church Without Walls movement, including its historical background, theological underpinnings, and practical implementation.

By studying Church Without Walls, we can gain insights into how technology and social media are changing how we worship and connect with others in the modern world. We can also obtain a more in-depth grasp of how the Church Without Walls movement addresses the needs of those who may not feel comfortable attending a traditional church or may be geographically isolated.

Another essential goal of this study is to examine a Church Without Walls's potential benefits and challenges. For example, we can explore how the Church Without Walls movement reaches new people and provides opportunities for spiritual growth and community building. We can also examine the challenges of maintaining relationships and providing pastoral care in a decentralized and non-traditional setting.

Overall, this study aims to provide a comprehensive understanding of the Church Without Walls movement and explore its implications for modern Christianity. By doing so, we can gain insights into how churches can adapt and evolve to meet the needs of an increasingly connected and diverse world. This study can also provide guidance for those who could be interested in establishing Church Without Walls, and those who are curious about this emerging trend in modern Christianity.

CHAPTER TWO

Biblical Basis Of Church Without Walls

The concept of a Church Without Walls has a strong Biblical basis, with many examples in the Bible's Old and New Testaments that emphasize the importance of community, worship, and outreach beyond the physical walls of a traditional church.

In the Old Testament, we see worship and community building in various settings, including homes and other non-traditional spaces. For example, in Exodus 18, we see Moses receiving advice from his father-in-law on delegating authority and organizing the people of Israel for worship and community building. This advice includes a suggestion to gather the people in small groups, which could be seen as an early example of the decentralized approach of a Church Without Walls.

In the New Testament, we see numerous examples of Jesus and his disciples engaging in worship, teaching, and community building outside the traditional synagogue or temple. For example, in Matthew 18:20, Jesus states, "For where two or three are gathered in my name, there am I among them." This verse highlights the importance of gathering in small groups and emphasizes the presence of God even in non-traditional worship settings.

Additionally, the Book of Acts provides many examples of the early Christian church gathering in homes and other non-traditional spaces for worship, prayer, and community building. Acts 2:42-47 describes the early church as "devoted to the apostles' teaching and to fellowship, to the breaking of bread and to prayer," with members meeting regularly in each other's homes.

The Apostle Paul also emphasizes the importance of community building and outreach in his letters to various early Christian communities. In 1 Corinthians 12, Paul describes the church as a body, with each member playing a unique role in the overall health and function of the body.

Overall, the Biblical basis of a Church Without Walls is rooted in the importance of community, worship, and outreach beyond physical walls. The examples in the Bible highlight the value of gathering in small groups, emphasizing the presence of God in non-traditional worship settings, and the importance of each member playing a unique role in the church's overall health.

The Great Commission

The Great Commission is a term used to describe the instructions given by Jesus to his disciples before his ascension into heaven, as recorded in the Gospel of Matthew 28:18-20. The Great Commission is often cited as a central mission of the Christian faith and a call to spread the Gospel message to all nations.

The text of the Great Commission reads as follows:

"Then Jesus came to them and said, 'All authority in heaven and on earth has been given to me. Therefore, go and make disciples of all nations, baptizing them in the name of the Father, Son, and the Holy Spirit, and teaching them to obey everything I have commanded you. And surely I am with you always, to the very end of the age.'"

The Great Commission is significant for several reasons. First, it emphasizes the universal scope of the Christian message, calling on believers to spread the Gospel to all nations. This highlights that Christianity is not limited to one particular culture or group of people but is a relevant message applicable to all people.

Second, the Great Commission emphasizes the importance of making disciples, not just converts. This means that Christians are called to share the Gospel message, help others grow in their faith, and develop a deeper understanding of what it means to follow Christ.

Finally, the Great Commission emphasizes the presence of Jesus with his disciples even as they go out into the world to spread the Gospel message. This highlights the idea that Christians are not alone in their mission but are supported by the presence and power of Jesus.

Overall, the Great Commission is a central mission of the Christian faith, calling on believers to spread the Gospel message to all nations, make disciples, and rely on the presence and power of Jesus in their mission. It is a call to action for Christians to share the love and message of Jesus with the world around them.

The Ministry Of Jesus

> *"Jesus went throughout Galilee, teaching in their synagogues, proclaiming the good news of the kingdom, and healing every disease and sickness among the people"* (Matthew 4:23).

The Ministry of Jesus refers to the three-year period in which Jesus Christ performed his public ministry before his crucifixion and resurrection. The ministry of Jesus is significant for several reasons, including how it fulfilled Old Testament prophecies about the coming of the Messiah, the miracles and teachings he performed that demonstrate his divine power and authority, and how it continues to shape the beliefs and practices of the Christian faith.

> *"The Spirit of the Lord is on me, because he has anointed me to proclaim good news to the poor. He has sent me to proclaim freedom for the prisoners and recovery of sight for the blind, to set the oppressed free"* (Luke 4:18).

Jesus performed numerous miracles during his ministry, including healing the sick, feeding the hungry, and raising the dead. These miracles demonstrated his divine power and authority, pointed people toward God, and gave them hope amid their suffering.

In addition to his miracles, Jesus also spent significant time teaching and preaching. He used parables and stories to communicate important spiritual truths to his followers and emphasized the importance of love, forgiveness, and compassion toward others.

One of the central themes of Jesus' ministry was his emphasis on the Kingdom of God. He taught that the Kingdom of God was not a physical place but rather a spiritual reality that could be experienced in the hearts of believers. He also emphasized the importance of repentance and turning away from sin to enter the Kingdom of God.

The Ministry of Jesus was characterized by his divine power and authority, emphasis on love, compassion, forgiveness, and teachings on the Kingdom of God. His ministry continues to shape the beliefs and practices of the Christian faith and serves as a reminder of the love and grace of God towards all people.

Learning From The Early Church Model

> *"All the believers were together and had everything in common. They sold property and possessions to give to anyone who had need. Every day they continued to meet together in the temple courts. They broke bread in their homes and ate together with glad and sincere hearts"* (Acts 2:44-46).

The Early Church Model refers to how the early Christian church operated and functioned in the first few centuries after the death and resurrection of Jesus Christ. This significant model provides insight into how Christianity developed and spread in its earliest stages. It can serve as inspiration and guidance for modern Christian communities.

One of the key characteristics of the Early Church Model was its emphasis on community and fellowship. Christians gathered together regularly for worship, prayer, and meal sharing. This sense of community was important because it supported and encouraged believers facing persecution and other challenges.

Another important aspect of the Early Church Model was its emphasis on discipleship and mentoring. Older, more experienced believers would mentor and disciple younger, less experienced believers, helping them to grow in their faith and develop a deeper understanding of the teachings of Jesus.

> *"Do nothing out of selfish ambition or vain conceit. Rather, in humility value others above yourselves, not looking to your own interests but each of you to the interests of the others" (Philippians 2:3-4).*

The Early Church Model was also characterized by its simplicity and humility. Believers were not focused on material possessions or status but on living a life pleasing to God and serving others.

Finally, the Early Church Model was marked by a sense of mission and purpose. Christians were committed to sharing the Gospel message with others and spreading the message of salvation to all nations. This sense of mission helped to drive the growth and expansion of the early Christian church.

Overall, the Early Church Model provides an inspiring and challenging example of what a Christian community and mission can look like. By focusing on community, discipleship, simplicity, and mission, modern Christian communities can seek to emulate the early Christian church and continue spreading the Gospel message to all people.

Applying Early Church Model To Modern Era

The Early Church model can provide useful insights for the modern era, but it is important to recognize that it needs to be adapted to contemporary circumstances.

One key relevant aspect of the Early Church model is its emphasis on community and fellowship. Early Christians valued gathering together, sharing meals, and supporting one another in need. In today's world, this can be applied through the formation of intentional communities and the cultivation of strong relationships within local churches. The internet and social media also provide new opportunities for creating virtual communities that can provide support and fellowship to people in different parts of the world.

Another important aspect of the Early Church model is its focus on simplicity and humility. Early Christians placed little value on material possessions or status, instead prioritizing a life of service to others. Today, this can be applied through minimalism and a commitment to serving others through acts of kindness and generosity. We can cultivate a deeper sense of purpose and meaning by seeking to live with less and give more.

The Early Church model also highlights the importance of evangelism and spreading the Gospel message. Early Christians were dedicated to sharing their faith with others and bringing new people into the community of believers. In the modern era, this can be applied through various forms of outreach, such as social media, community service, and personal relationships. However, it is important to remember that effective evangelism requires a deep understanding of the culture and context in which we are operating and must be approached with sensitivity and respect.

Finally, the Early Church model emphasizes the importance of unity within the church. Despite their diverse backgrounds and perspectives, early Christians were able to come together under a shared belief in Jesus Christ. In the modern era, it is important to remember that despite our differences, we are all part of the same body of Christ and must work together towards a common goal. By striving for unity and seeking to understand and respect one another, we can build stronger communities and work towards a brighter future.

While the Early Church model needs to be adapted to the modern era, its emphasis on community, simplicity, evangelism, and unity is very important. We can create a better world for ourselves and future generations by incorporating these principles into our lives and communities.

CHAPTER THREE

Characteristics Of A Church Without Walls

A Church Without Walls is a Christian community that seeks to break down the barriers between the church and the world and create a sense of community and fellowship that is open to all people, regardless of their background or beliefs. Several key characteristics define a Church Without Walls:

- **Inclusivity:** A Church Without Walls is open to all people, regardless of race, ethnicity, gender, or social status. It seeks to create a sense of community that is welcoming and accepting of everyone and actively seeks out those marginalized or excluded by society.

- **Relational:** A Church Without Walls emphasizes the importance of relationships and personal connections. It seeks to create a sense of community built on trust, respect, and mutual support, and it encourages its members to build meaningful relationships with one another.

- **Service-oriented:** A Church Without Walls is committed to serving others and meeting the needs of its community. It may engage in acts of service, such as volunteering at local shelters or food banks, or organize events that benefit the community, such as neighborhood clean-up days.

- **Christ-centered:** A Church Without Walls is rooted in the teachings and example of Jesus Christ. It seeks to follow his example of love, compassion, and self-sacrifice, emphasizing the importance of personal faith and spiritual growth.

- **Innovative:** A Church Without Walls is willing to try new things and take risks to reach out to its community. It may use social media or other forms of technology to connect with people or experiment with new forms of worship or community outreach.

- A Church Without Walls is characterized by its commitment to inclusivity, flexibility, relationality, service, Christ-centeredness, and innovation. Embodying these characteristics can create a vibrant and dynamic community that is open to all people and dedicated to serving others in the name of Jesus Christ.

Openness To All

Openness to all is a key characteristic of a Church Without Walls. It means the church is open and welcoming to people of all backgrounds, regardless of race, ethnicity, gender, sexual orientation, socioeconomic status, or religious affiliation.

This openness to all is rooted in the teachings of Jesus Christ, who welcomed and embraced all people, regardless of their status or background. Jesus' message of love and acceptance is a central theme in the Christian faith and is the foundation of the Church Without Walls.

By being open to all, the Church Without Walls creates an inclusive and accepting environment. It creates a sense of community that is built on the principles of love, respect, and mutual support, and it seeks to create a safe and welcoming space for everyone.

Openness to all also means that the Church Without Walls is committed to breaking down the barriers that separate people from one another. It seeks to bridge the gap between the church and the world and to create a sense of connection and community that extends beyond the walls of the church building.

Overall, openness to all is a core value of the Church Without Walls. It is essential for creating a vibrant and dynamic community committed to serving others in the name of Jesus Christ.

Emphasis On Discipleship

Emphasis on discipleship is a critical characteristic of a Church Without Walls. Discipleship is the process of growing in faith and following the teachings of Jesus Christ. The Church Without Walls emphasizes discipleship because it recognizes that spiritual growth is an ongoing process that requires intentional effort and commitment.

"Iron sharpens iron, and one man sharpens another." - Proverbs 27:17

One of the key ways that the Church Without Walls emphasizes discipleship is through teaching and learning. The church provides opportunities for its members to study the Bible, learn about Christian theology, and engage in discussions about faith and spirituality. This emphasis on education and learning helps members grow in their faith and deepen their understanding of the teachings of Jesus Christ.

Another way that the Church Without Walls emphasizes discipleship is through mentorship and accountability. Church members are encouraged to form relationships with one another and support each other in their spiritual journeys. This can take the form of one-on-one mentorship, small group accountability, or other forms of community support.

"For even the Son of Man came not to be served but to serve, and to give his life as a ransom for many." - Mark 10:45

The Church Without Walls also emphasizes the importance of service and outreach as key aspect of discipleship. By serving others and sharing the love of Jesus Christ with those in need, church members can put their faith into action and live out the teachings of Jesus.

Overall, the Church Without Walls emphasizes discipleship greatly because it recognizes that spiritual growth is essential for building a strong and vibrant community of faith. By prioritizing teaching and learning, mentorship and accountability, and service and outreach, the church can create a supportive and empowering environment that helps its members grow in their faith and become more like Jesus Christ.

Use Of Technology

The use of technology is an important characteristic of a Church Without Walls. With technological advances, the church can reach a broader audience and engage with people in new and innovative ways. Here are some ways in which technology is used in the context of a Church Without Walls:

- **Online Worship Services:** The church can use technology to offer online worship services, allowing people to participate in worship from their homes. This is particularly important for people unable to attend in-person services due to distance, mobility issues, or other factors.

- **Social Media:** Social media platforms such as Facebook, Instagram, and Twitter can be used to share information about the church and upcoming events and engage with congregation members. Social media can also be used to reach out to people not currently connected with the church and to share the gospel's message with them.

- **Podcasts and Online Teaching:** The church can use podcasts, video sermons, and online teaching to allow members to learn and grow in their faith outside traditional worship services. This can be particularly useful for people unable to attend in-person teaching due to scheduling conflicts or other factors.

- **Virtual Small Groups:** The use of video conferencing technology such as Zoom or Skype can allow church members to connect with each other in virtual small groups, even if they cannot meet in person. This can be a great way to build community and support each other in prayer and fellowship.

- **Online Giving:** Technology can be used to make it easy for church members to give financially, even if they cannot attend in-person services. This can be done through online giving platforms or mobile apps, making donating to the church simple and convenient.

Overall, the use of technology is an important characteristic of a Church Without Walls. By embracing new and innovative ways to connect with people, the church can reach a broader audience and create a more dynamic and engaged faith community.

Flexibility In Worship

Flexibility in worship is another key characteristic of a Church Without Walls. This means that the church is willing to adapt its worship style and practices to meet its members' needs and reach out to new audiences. Here are some ways in which a Church Without Walls can demonstrate flexibility in worship:

- **Multiple Worship Styles:** The church can offer multiple worship styles, such as traditional, contemporary, or blended, to appeal to a diverse group of people. This can be particularly important for younger generations, who may prefer a more contemporary style of worship.

- **Alternative Worship Venues:** The church can hold worship services in alternative venues, such as outdoor locations or community centers, to reach people who may not feel comfortable in a traditional church setting.

- **Creative Worship Elements:** The church can incorporate creative worship elements, such as drama, dance, or visual arts, to engage people in new and innovative ways.

- **Flexible Service Times:** The church can offer worship services at flexible times, such as in the evening or on weekends, to accommodate the schedules of its members.

- **Intergenerational Worship:** The church can create intergenerational worship experiences, bringing people of all ages together in worship and fellowship.

Overall, flexibility in worship is an important characteristic of a Church Without Walls. By being open to new ideas and willing to adapt its worship practices, the church can create a welcoming and inclusive environment that meets the needs of its members and reaches out to new audiences.

Social Justice And Outreach

Social justice and outreach are important characteristics of a Church Without Walls. The church is called to be a force for positive change in the world, including advocating for social justice and serving the community's needs.

Here are some ways in which a Church Without Walls can demonstrate a commitment to social justice and outreach:

- **Community Service:** The church can engage in community service projects, such as volunteering at a local food bank or homeless shelter, to meet the needs of the less fortunate.

- **Advocacy:** The church can advocate for social justice issues, such as ending poverty, promoting racial justice, or advocating for the rights of the marginalized.

- **Environmental Stewardship:** The church can promote environmental stewardship and encourage members to take actions that protect the planet.

- **Mission Trips:** The church can organize mission trips to other parts of the country or world to serve the needs of people in other communities.

- **Partnerships:** The church can partner with local organizations and other churches to amplify its impact and create a support network for those in need.

Overall, a commitment to social justice and outreach is an important characteristic of a Church Without Walls. By engaging in community service, advocating for social justice issues, and serving the needs of others, the church can positively impact the world and demonstrate the love of Christ to those around us.

CHAPTER FOUR

Benefits Of Church Without Walls

Several benefits to a Church Without Walls make it an attractive option for many people. Here are some of the key benefits:

- **Increased Accessibility:** A Church Without Walls is often more accessible to people who cannot attend a traditional church due to mobility issues, transportation challenges, or other barriers. Using technology and alternative venues, the church can reach a wider audience and create a more inclusive community.

- **Community Outreach:** A Church Without Walls often strongly emphasizes community outreach and social justice issues. By engaging in service projects and advocating for social justice, the church can make a positive impact on the world and demonstrate the love of Christ to those around us.

- **Discipleship:** A Church Without Walls often strongly emphasizes discipleship, providing opportunities for members to grow in their faith and connect with others on a deeper level. This can lead to a more meaningful and fulfilling spiritual journey.

A Church Without Walls can benefit its members and the wider community. By creating a more accessible, flexible, and socially engaged community, the church can help people grow in their faith and positively impact the world.

Accessibility

Accessibility is an important benefit of a Church Without Walls. Due to mobility issues, transportation challenges, or other barriers, traditional churches may be difficult or impossible for some people to attend. A Church Without Walls can use technology and alternative venues to create a more accessible worship experience.

For example, the church may offer online services or transportation to off-site locations. This can allow people unable to attend a traditional church due to mobility issues or lack of transportation to participate in worship and community activities. Additionally, technology can enable people to connect with the church community from anywhere in the world, making the church more accessible to people who are geographically isolated or have other barriers to attending in-person services.

By creating a more accessible worship experience, a Church Without Walls can create a more inclusive community that welcomes people of all backgrounds and abilities. This can help to break down barriers and create a more connected and supportive community, allowing people to grow in their faith and connect with others on a deeper level.

Overall, accessibility is an important benefit of a Church Without Walls that can make worship and community activities more inclusive and welcoming to people who may have difficulty attending a traditional church.

Diversity

Diversity is a key benefit of a Church Without Walls. Traditional churches may be limited in their ability to attract a diverse range of people due to factors such as location, worship style, or cultural traditions. A Church Without Walls, on the other hand, can use technology and alternative venues to create a more diverse and inclusive community.

By offering online services and using social media, Church Without Walls can reach people worldwide and from various cultural, ethnic, and linguistic backgrounds. Additionally, using alternative venues such as community centers, parks, and other public spaces, the church can create a more welcoming and accessible environment for people from different backgrounds.

A Church Without Walls can also create a more diverse community by offering a variety of worship styles and incorporating different cultural traditions into its services. This can help to break down cultural barriers and create a more inclusive and welcoming environment for people from all backgrounds.

Overall, diversity is an important benefit of a Church Without Walls that can create a more inclusive and welcoming community. By attracting people from various backgrounds and offering a range of worship styles and cultural traditions, the church can create a more vibrant and dynamic community that can better connect with people and meet their spiritual needs.

Cost-Effective

Another benefit of a Church Without Walls is that it can be cost-effective. Traditional churches often have significant overhead costs, such as building maintenance, utility bills, and salaries for staff members. These costs can limit the resources available for outreach and community activities.

In contrast, a Church Without Walls can operate with significantly lower overhead costs. Using technology and alternative venues, the church can reduce or eliminate the need for a physical building, saving money on rent, utilities, and maintenance. Additionally, the church can use volunteers to help with administrative tasks and community outreach, reducing the need for paid staff members.

The cost savings associated with a Church Without Walls can allow the church to invest more resources in outreach and community activities. For example, the church may be able to offer more extensive community services, such as food banks, homeless shelters, or addiction support programs. Additionally, the church may be able to provide more financial support to local charities and community organizations.

Overall, the cost-effectiveness of a Church Without Walls can allow the church to have a greater impact on its community and better serve the needs of its members. The church can create a more dynamic and impactful ministry by reducing overhead costs and investing resources in outreach and community activities.

Community Building

Community building is a significant benefit of a Church Without Walls. Using technology and alternative venues, the church can create a more connected and supportive community that extends beyond the walls of a traditional church building.

A Church Without Walls can create opportunities for people to connect and engage with one another outside of traditional worship services through online platforms and social media. This can include online prayer groups, Bible studies, and social activities. Using technology, the church can connect people worldwide who share common interests and beliefs.

Additionally, a Church Without Walls can use alternative venues to create a more inclusive and welcoming environment for community activities. For example, the church may organize events in local parks, community centers, or other public spaces, making it easier for people to participate in community activities without feeling intimidated or overwhelmed by a traditional church environment.

By creating a more connected and supportive community, a Church Without Walls can help to build stronger relationships among members and foster a sense of belonging and shared purpose. This can help to support people in their faith journey and create a more vibrant and dynamic church community.

Overall, community building is an important benefit of a Church Without Walls that can create a more connected and supportive community beyond the walls of a traditional church building. Using technology and alternative venues, the church can create opportunities for people to connect and engage with one another, strengthening relationships and fostering a sense of belonging and shared purpose.

CHAPTER FIVE

Challenges Of Church Without Walls

Although Church Without Walls has many benefits, several challenges must be addressed. Here are some of the challenges that a Church Without Walls may face:

- **Lack of physical presence** - A Church Without Walls may struggle to establish a physical presence in the community. This can make it difficult to build relationships and reach out to people not already part of the church community.

- **Technical difficulties** - A Church Without Walls relies heavily on technology to connect with members and to provide worship services. Technical difficulties, such as internet outages or equipment failure, can disrupt the worship experience and make it challenging for members to participate.

- **Isolation** - A Church Without Walls may be more prone to isolation than a traditional church. Members may feel disconnected from one another if they cannot attend in-person worship services or events.

- **Limited resources** - A Church Without Walls may have limited resources regarding finances and personnel. This can make it challenging to provide the level of pastoral care and outreach that a traditional church may offer.

- **Resistance to change** - Some members may resist the idea of a Church Without Walls, preferring a more traditional church experience. It may take time to convince members to embrace this new ministry model.

A Church Without Walls must be prepared to address these challenges to thrive. By developing strategies to overcome isolation, technical difficulties, and accountability issues and communicating the benefits of this ministry model, a Church Without Walls can successfully navigate these challenges and continue to grow and thrive.

Maintaining Relationships

Maintaining relationships is essential to any church community, but it can be particularly challenging for a Church Without Walls. Without a physical building or regular in-person gatherings, establishing and maintaining meaningful relationships between members can be more difficult.

Here are some strategies that can help a Church Without Walls maintain strong relationships:

- **Emphasize small groups** - Small groups can effectively build relationships within a Church Without Walls. By creating smaller, more intimate communities, members can connect more deeply with one another and provide mutual support and accountability.

- **Encourage communication** - Communication is key to maintaining relationships, so it's important to encourage regular communication between members. This can be facilitated through messaging apps, social media groups, or other online platforms.

- **Host regular events** - While a Church Without Walls may not have a physical building, it can still host regular events that unite members. These events can be hosted in public spaces or online, including worship services, social gatherings, and outreach events.

- **Prioritize pastoral care** - Pastoral care is essential to maintaining relationships within a church community. A Church Without Walls should prioritize pastoral care by ensuring members have access to counseling, prayer, and other forms of support.

- **Foster a sense of community** - A Church Without Walls can foster a sense of community by emphasizing shared values, creating a strong brand identity, and encouraging members to participate in outreach events that benefit the wider community.

By implementing these strategies, a Church Without Walls can maintain strong relationships between members and foster a sense of community essential to its success.

Providing Pastoral Care

Providing pastoral care is an important aspect of any church community, including a Church Without Walls. Pastoral care refers to the emotional and spiritual support that church community members provide to one another during times of need or difficulty. This support can include counseling, prayer, and other forms of support that help members navigate challenging situations.

Here are some strategies that a Church Without Walls can use to provide effective pastoral care:

- **Train pastoral care providers** - A Church Without Walls should train members to provide pastoral care. These individuals should deeply understand the community's needs and be able to provide effective emotional and spiritual support.

- **Offer counseling services** - Counseling services can be an effective way to provide pastoral care to members. A Church Without Walls can partner with trained counselors or offer counseling services through trained community members.

- **Provide prayer support** - Prayer is an important aspect of pastoral care, and a Church Without Walls can provide prayer support through online prayer groups or prayer chains.

- **Create support groups** - Support groups can be an effective way to provide pastoral care to members who are going through similar challenges. A Church Without Walls can create support groups for individuals dealing with addiction, grief, or other challenges.

- **Foster a culture of support** - A Church Without Walls can foster a culture of support by encouraging members to be open and honest about their struggles and providing opportunities for members to support one another.

By providing effective pastoral care, a Church Without Walls can create a supportive community that helps members navigate life's challenges and grow in their faith.

Financial Sustainability

Financial sustainability, including a Church Without Walls, is an important challenge for any church community. A Church Without Walls needs to generate income and manage its expenses to sustain its operations. Here are some strategies that a Church Without Walls can use to achieve financial sustainability:

- **Diversify income sources:** A Church Without Walls can generate income from various sources, including donations, grants, and events or programs. By diversifying its income sources, Church Without Walls can reduce its reliance on any one source of funding.

- **Create a budget:** A Church Without Walls should create a budget that outlines their expected income and expenses. This budget should be reviewed regularly and adjusted to ensure that the Church Without Walls remains financially sustainable.

- **Manage expenses effectively:** A Church Without Walls should manage its expenses carefully to ensure they use its resources effectively. This can involve negotiating with vendors for better prices, reducing unnecessary expenses, and finding efficient ways to operate.

By implementing these strategies, Church Without Walls can achieve financial sustainability and continue to serve its community effectively. It's important to note that financial sustainability is an ongoing process. The Church Without Walls will need to continue to adapt and evolve its strategies over time to remain financially viable.

Accountability

Accountability is a key component of any successful Church Without Walls. Since a Church Without Walls is often decentralized and operates without a physical building, it is important to have mechanisms to ensure that everyone involved is accountable to each other and the community they serve. Here are some strategies that a Church Without Walls can use to promote accountability:

- **Define clear roles and responsibilities:** A Church Without Walls should clearly define the roles and responsibilities of each community member. This can help to ensure that everyone understands their responsibilities and is held accountable for their actions.

- **Establish communication channels:** A Church Without Walls should establish clear and effective communication channels to ensure that everyone is informed about what is happening within the community. This can include regular meetings, newsletters, social media updates, or other methods of communication.

- **Develop a code of conduct:** A Church Without Walls should develop a code of conduct that outlines the community's behavior expectations. This code should be communicated to all members and enforced consistently to promote accountability.

- **Implement a system for addressing grievances:** A Church Without Walls should have a system for addressing grievances or conflicts that may arise within the community. This can include a grievance procedure, mediation, or other dispute resolution mechanisms.

- **Conduct regular evaluations:** A Church Without Walls should regularly evaluate its activities and programs to ensure they meet their goals and serve the community effectively. This can help to identify areas for improvement and promote accountability.

By implementing these strategies, a Church Without Walls can promote accountability and ensure everyone involved is working towards the common goal of serving the community. It is important to note that accountability is an ongoing process. The Church Without Walls will need to continue to adapt and evolve its strategies over time to remain effective.

CHAPTER SIX

Case Studies Of Church Without Walls

Case studies of Church Without Walls can provide valuable insights into this ministry model's practical implementation and benefits. Here are a few examples:

LifeChurch.tv - LifeChurch.tv is a non-denominational Church Without Walls that operates primarily through its online platform. The Church offers live streaming of worship services, online Bible studies, and prayer groups. Additionally, the Church provides an online community platform that allows members to connect with one another and participate in small group discussions. LifeChurch.tv has a global audience and has reached people who might not otherwise attend a traditional church.

St. Isidore's Episcopal Church - St. Isidore's Episcopal Church is an example of a Church Without Walls that operates through a network of house churches. The Church is located in Houston, Texas, and offers traditional Sunday worship services and a network of small house churches that meet throughout the week. The house churches provide an intimate and supportive environment for members to connect and engage with one another. In contrast, the traditional worship services provide a more ample gathering space for the entire community.

Elevation Church - Elevation Church is a non-denominational Church Without Walls that operates through a network of physical locations and online platforms. The Church has physical locations in multiple states and offers online worship services, Bible studies, and community groups. The Church strongly emphasizes community outreach and has successfully engaged with local communities through programs such as food banks and homeless shelters.

These case studies demonstrate the variety of ways that Church Without Walls can be implemented, from purely online platforms to a network of physical locations and house churches. Additionally, these case studies highlight the benefits of Church Without Walls, including increased accessibility, community building, and outreach opportunities.

Saddleback Online

Saddleback Online is the ministry of Saddleback Church, a megachurch in Southern California. Saddleback Online was established in 2004 to reach people unable to attend physical church services. The ministry has grown significantly since its inception and now reaches thousands worldwide.

Saddleback Online offers various services and resources to support people's faith journey. Some of the key offerings include:

- **Online worship services:** Saddleback Online broadcasts its weekend services online, allowing people to participate in worship and listen to sermons from anywhere in the world.

- **Small groups:** Saddleback Online offers online small groups, providing opportunities for people to connect with others, discuss faith, and support each other.

- **Online courses:** Saddleback Online offers a range of online courses covering topics such as biblical studies, personal growth, and leadership development.

- **Counseling services:** Saddleback Online offers online counseling services, providing support and guidance to people dealing with various issues, including mental health, addiction, and relationship problems.

- **Prayer and support:** Saddleback Online provides online prayer support, connecting people with trained volunteers who can offer prayer and support.

Saddleback Online has successfully reached people unable to attend physical church services due to geographical or other constraints. The ministry has also effectively created a sense of community and supported people through its various online offerings. Saddleback Online is an example of how technology can help the Church Without Walls model and reach people who may not otherwise have access to traditional church services.

Life.Church

Life. Church is a multisite church headquartered in Edmond, Oklahoma. The Church was founded in 1996 by Craig Groeschel and has since grown to become one of the largest churches in the United States, with over 30 physical locations in 10 states.

In addition to its physical locations, Life.Church has also developed a significant online presence through its Life.Church Online platform. Life.Church Online offers a variety of online services and resources, including:

- **Online worship services:** Life.Church Online broadcasts its weekend services online, allowing people to participate in worship and listen to sermons from anywhere in the world.

- **Church Online Platform:** Life.Church has developed a proprietary Church Online Platform that enables churches to create and host online services and resources.

- **Bible App:** Life.Church has also developed a popular Bible App, downloaded over 400 million times worldwide. The app provides access to various translations, devotional plans, and other resources to support people in their faith journey.

- **Online courses:** Life.Church Online offers a range of online courses covering topics such as marriage, parenting, and personal finance.

- **Online community:** Life.Church Online allows people to connect with others and build community through online chat rooms and discussion boards.

Life.Church has successfully used technology to support its mission of reaching people and helping them grow in their faith. The Church's use of the Church Online Platform has enabled other churches to benefit from its technology and get people in their communities. Life.Church is an example of how technology can support the Church Without Walls model and expand the Church's reach beyond physical locations.

Mennonite Online Fellowship

Mennonite Online Fellowship is an online community founded in 2008 by a group of Mennonites who wanted to provide a space to connect and build a community outside traditional physical church buildings. The community is not affiliated with any specific denomination but is rooted in the Anabaptist tradition of Christianity.

Mennonite Online Fellowship offers a variety of online resources and services to support its members, including:

- **Online worship services:** Mennonite Online Fellowship hosts regular online worship services, which include music, prayer, and a sermon. Members can participate in the service from anywhere in the world.

- **Online Bible studies:** The community also hosts online Bible studies, which allow members to engage with scripture and discuss their faith with others.

- **Online discussion forums:** Mennonite Online Fellowship has online discussion forums where members can connect with others, share their experiences, and support one another.

- **Online prayer requests:** Members can submit prayer requests online, which are then shared with the community so that others can pray for them.

Mennonite Online Fellowship has successfully used technology to support its mission of building community and providing spiritual support to its members. The community has provided a space for people who may not have access to a physical church building or prefer to connect online to participate in worship, engage with scripture, and build relationships with others. Mennonite Online Fellowship exemplifies how the Church Without Walls model can support and enhance traditional structures.

St. Isidore's Episcopal Church

St. Isidore's Episcopal Church is an example of a physical church community that has embraced the Church Without Walls model by utilizing technology to reach a broader audience and expand its outreach.

Located in Texas, St. Isidore's Episcopal Church offers a variety of online resources and services to support its members and connect with those who may not be able to attend physical services. Some of the online resources and services offered by the Church include:

- **Live streaming services:** St. Isidore's Episcopal Church live streams its services, allowing anyone to participate in worship from anywhere in the world.

- **Online prayer requests:** Members and non-members can submit prayer requests online, which are shared with the church community so that others can pray for them.

- **Online Bible studies:** The Church offers online Bible studies, which allow members to engage with scripture and discuss their faith with others.

- **Online giving:** St. Isidore's Episcopal Church offers online giving options, allowing members to tithe and donate to the Church electronically.

By embracing the Church Without Walls model, St. Isidore's Episcopal Church has been able to reach a wider audience and connect with people who may not have access to a physical church community. The Church has successfully used technology to expand its outreach and provide spiritual support to its members and the broader community.

CHAPTER SEVEN

Impact Of Church Without Walls

The impact of Church Without Walls has been significant in several ways:

- **Increased Accessibility:** Church Without Walls has made it possible for people who may not have been able to attend traditional church services to participate in worship and engage with their faith. This includes people with physical disabilities, those living in remote areas, and those who cannot attend church for other reasons.

- **Greater Diversity:** Church Without Walls has also brought greater diversity to the church community. Using technology to reach a wider audience, churches can connect with people from different backgrounds, cultures, and communities.

- **Expanded Outreach:** Church Without Walls has also expanded the outreach of the church community. By using technology to reach people beyond the local community, churches can spread their message and connect with people who may not have been reached otherwise.

- **Enhanced Discipleship:** Church Without Walls has also enhanced discipleship by providing online Bible studies, discipleship classes, and other resources that allow people to deepen their faith and grow in their relationship with God.

- **Increased Flexibility:** Church Without Walls has also increased the flexibility of church services. By providing online resources, churches can offer worship services and other events at different times and formats to accommodate their members' needs.

Overall, the impact of Church Without Walls has been significant in making the church community more accessible, diverse, and inclusive. It has expanded the church's outreach and enhanced discipleship opportunities for those who may not have been able to participate otherwise.

Increased Reach

Yes, Church Without Walls has definitely increased the reach of the church. By using technology and online platforms, churches can now connect with people worldwide, expanding their outreach and sharing their message with a much wider audience. This has been particularly helpful during times of crisis, such as the COVID-19 pandemic, when traditional forms of gathering and worship have been limited. Church Without Walls had allowed churches to continue providing spiritual support and resources to their members, even when physical gatherings were impossible. Additionally, the increased reach of Church Without Walls has made it possible for people who may have felt disconnected or isolated from traditional church communities to find a place of belonging and connect with other believers.

Changed Lives

Church Without Walls has also had a significant impact on changing lives. By providing accessible and flexible ways for people to engage with their faith, Church Without Walls has made it possible for individuals who may not have been able to attend traditional church services to connect with God and find spiritual fulfillment. The emphasis on discipleship in Church Without Walls has also helped individuals deepen their relationship with Christ and develop a stronger understanding of their faith. Many people have found a sense of community and support through online church communities, leading to positive changes in their lives, including improved mental health and a greater sense of purpose and meaning. The convenience and accessibility of Church Without Walls have also allowed individuals to integrate their faith into their daily lives, leading to a more holistic and integrated approach to spirituality.

Community Impact

Church Without Walls has also had a significant impact on the community at large. By using online platforms and technology, churches can reach a broader audience and connect with people from diverse backgrounds and cultures. This has led to more inclusive and diverse communities of faith, which has positively impacted both the church and the wider community. Church Without Walls has also provided practical support to those in need through online counseling services, support groups, and outreach programs. This has helped to build stronger and more resilient communities, as individuals are supported in times of need and given the resources and tools to navigate life's challenges. Additionally, Church Without Walls has provided a platform for churches to raise awareness and advocate for social justice issues, such as poverty, racism, and inequality. By mobilizing their online communities, churches have been able to effect positive change and make a meaningful impact on the world around them.

CHAPTER EIGHT

Future Of Church Without Walls

The future of Church Without Walls is bright, as more and more churches recognize the need for accessible and flexible ways for people to engage with their faith. As technology advances, churches will have more opportunities to connect with people and build communities of faith online. This will allow churches to reach a broader audience and provide more resources and support to needy individuals. Additionally, the COVID-19 pandemic has accelerated the adoption of Church Without Walls, as many churches were forced to move their services and programs online due to social distancing measures. As a result, more people have become comfortable participating in church online, opening up new possibilities for the future of Church Without Walls.

However, some challenges come with the future of Church Without Walls. As online communities continue to grow, it will become increasingly important for churches to maintain a sense of authenticity and connection with their members. This will require creative approaches to community-building and pastoral care, as well as a commitment to building relationships and providing meaningful support to those in need. Additionally, as Church Without Walls continues to grow, there will be a need for greater accountability and transparency to ensure that churches are meeting the needs of their members and providing meaningful opportunities for spiritual growth and engagement.

Despite these challenges, the future of Church Without Walls holds great promise. It offers a unique opportunity for churches to connect with people in new and innovative ways and provide accessible and flexible opportunities for individuals to engage with their faith.

Emerging Trends

Emerging trends in Church Without Walls reflect the changing landscape of faith and technology. Here are some of the key trends to watch for in the coming years:

- **Virtual reality (VR) and augmented reality (AR):** As technology continues to evolve, VR and AR offer new opportunities for churches to create immersive and interactive online worship experiences.

- **Podcasting and audio content:** Podcasts have become a popular way for churches to share sermons, Bible studies, and other audio content with their members, providing an on-demand and accessible way for people to engage with their faith.

- **Social media and live streaming:** Social media platforms like Facebook and YouTube have become key tools for churches to reach new audiences and connect with their members online. Live streaming has become increasingly popular, allowing churches to broadcast services and events in real-time.

- **Online small groups and discipleship:** Online small groups and discipleship programs are becoming more popular, allowing people to connect with each other and grow in their faith from anywhere in the world.

- **Virtual reality and digital missions:** Virtual reality and digital missions offer new opportunities for churches to engage in outreach and evangelism by creating online spaces for people to explore and learn about faith.

These emerging trends reflect the continued evolution of Church Without Walls, as churches seek new and innovative ways to connect with people and build faith communities online.

Opportunities

The opportunities of Church Without Walls are numerous and exciting. Here are some of the key opportunities that this model of the church presents:

- **Increased reach:** Church Without Walls allows churches to reach people who might not otherwise attend a physical church, including those who live far away, have disabilities or health issues, or have busy schedules.

- **Flexibility and convenience:** Online church services and events can be accessed from anywhere with an internet connection, making it easier for people to fit worship and fellowship into their busy lives.

- **Innovation and creativity:** Church Without Walls allows churches to experiment with new forms of worship, outreach, and discipleship that might not be possible in a traditional church setting.

- **Access to resources:** Online communities of faith can connect people to a wealth of resources, including Bible studies, devotions, and online courses that can help them grow in their faith.

- **Collaboration and networking:** Church Without Walls can facilitate collaboration and networking between churches and faith communities worldwide, allowing people to learn from each other and work together to achieve common goals.

Overall, Church Without Walls presents numerous opportunities for churches and faith communities to expand their reach, engage with new audiences, and experiment with new forms of worship and outreach.

Threats

While there are many opportunities associated with the Church Without Walls model, there are also several potential threats that churches should be aware of. Here are some of the key threats to consider:

- **Loss of community:** One of the biggest challenges of the online church is maintaining a sense of community and connection between members. Without face-to-face interaction, building meaningful relationships and establishing a sense of belonging can be difficult.

- **Online security:** Online communities are vulnerable to cyber-attacks and other security threats, which can compromise the safety and privacy of members.

- **Technology barriers:** Not everyone has access to the internet or the technology required to participate in online church activities, which can limit the church's reach.

- **Decreased engagement:** Some people may be more likely to disengage from church activities if they only participate online, as ignoring or disengaging from virtual events can be easier.

- **Financial sustainability:** Church Without Walls requires investment in technology and other resources, which can be costly and challenging to sustain over the long term.

Overall, while Church Without Walls presents many opportunities for churches, it is important to be aware of these potential threats and to take steps to mitigate them to ensure the success and sustainability of this church model.

Conclusion

In conclusion, the Church Without Walls model is a growing trend in modern-day Christianity that presents opportunities and challenges for churches. By embracing technology, promoting inclusivity, and prioritizing discipleship and outreach, churches can effectively leverage the benefits of this model to reach a wider audience and have a greater impact in their communities. However, it is also important for churches to be aware of the potential challenges and threats associated with this model, such as the loss of community, technology barriers, and financial sustainability. By proactively addressing these issues, churches can successfully navigate the changing landscape of modern-day Christianity and continue to fulfill their mission of spreading the gospel and serving their communities.

References:

The Power to Change - Laef FM Vanuatu. https://www.laeffm.org/2022/04/23/the-power-to-change/

The Importance of Christian Camps in Today's World - Bongiorno Christian Retreat Center. https://bongiornocc.com/the-importance-of-christian-camps-in-todays-world/

Leaders - Cornerstone Community Church.

http://www.cornerstonelacrosse.org/leaders/

Grace Students - South Overland Park | Grace Church KS Website.

https://visitgracechurch.com/event/1132

Understanding the impact of racial discrimination on adult health and wellbeing |

Health Research Council of New Zealand.

https://www.hrc.govt.nz/resources/research-repository/understanding-impact-racial-d

References

iscrimination-adult-health-and-wellbeing

Life Demonstration Church | Peter's Miraculous Escape from Prison.

https://lifedemonstration.com/peters-miraculous-escape-prison/

What does the bible say about reading books? - Sbooks. https://sbooks.org/faq/what-does-the-bible-say-about-reading-books/

To Be a Disciple Part 1. Matthew 28:18-20 (NIV) Then Jesus came to them and said, "All authority in heaven and on earth has been given to me. Therefore. - ppt download. https://slideplayer.com/slide/6110197/

WOP6 | Pptl. https://www.pptl.ca/copy-of-wop5

Matthew 4:22-24 - Proclaiming God's Word. https://proclaiming.com/2017/12/12/matthew-422-24/

Luke 4:18 "The Spirit of the Lord is on me, because he has anointed me to proclaim good news to the poor. He has sent me to proclaim freedom for the prisoners and recovery of sight for the blind, to set the oppressed free,. https://www.bibleapps.com/par/luke/4-18.htm

Early Church History | AllFearless Christian Ministries.

http://allfearless.com/2023/01/early-church-history/

References

January 1, 2022 - St. Patrick's Parish. https://www.saintpatrickkc.com/homilies/january-1-2022

Philippians 2:3-4: "Do nothing out of selfish ambition or vain conceit. Rather, in humility value others above yourselves, not looking to your own interests but each of you to the interests of the others." – Thought Of The Day. https://freeonline.blog/2019/09/18/philippians-23-4-do-nothing-out-of-selfish-ambiti on-or-vain-conceit-rather-in-humility-value-others-above-yourselves-not-looking-to-yo ur-own-interests-but-each-of-you-to-the-interests-of-the-ot/

merry memes - Page 252 — CIGAR.com Forum. https://forum.cigar.com/discussion/899184/merry-memes/p252